ULTIMATE

DARICE BAILER

The Child's World®
childsworld.com

Published by The Child's World®
1980 Lookout Drive • Mankato, MN 56003-1705
800-599-READ • www.childsworld.com

Photo Credits
© Aflo Co. Ltd./Alamy Stock Photo: 14-15; AP
Images/Ina Fassbender/picture-alliance/dpa: 6;
AP Images/Daily Gazette/Stacey Lauren-Kennedy:
18; AP Images/Niall Carson 17; Bob Daemmrich/
Alamy Stock Photo: 5; Brian Flaigmore/Dreamstime:
20-21; Lisa James/Napa Valley Register/ZUMA
Press Inc./Alamy Stock Photo: 13; PJF Military
Collection/Alamy Stock Photo/Alamy Stock Photo:
10; Steve Kingsman/Dreamstime/cover; US Air
Force: 9

ISBN: 9781503823754
LCCN: 2017944896

Printed in the United States of America
PA02356

ABOUT THE AUTHOR

Darice Bailer has wanted to be a writer since she was in fifth grade. Today she is the author of many books for young readers. She lives in Kansas with her husband.

TABLE OF CONTENTS

A FUN GAME OF KEEP AWAY

Do you like to run down a grassy field? Do you like to play keep away? Then Ultimate is an exciting game for you!

FUN FACT

In 1968, students invented Ultimate at Columbia High School in New Jersey.

The game of Ultimate looks a bit like football. But it's played with a round plastic **disc**. Some call the disc a **frisbee**.

Get ready to chase the disc as it flies. Leap high or dive low for a catch. Have fun under sunny skies.

FUN FACT

Grab your sneakers! Athletes run a lot during a game. Some players can run miles!

GAME ON!

Two teams play one another in Ultimate. Each team has seven players. Players pass the disc down the field. **Defenders** try to keep the other team's players from catching the disc.

No one can run with the disc. And throwers have just 10 seconds to pass the disc to someone else.

How do teams decide who throws first? Sometimes they play "rock-paper-scissors."

When a player catches a pass in the other team's **end zone**, his team scores a point. The team with the most points wins.

FUN FACT

Ultimate is played by millions of people all over the world.

SNAP AND THROW

Backhand is an easy throw to learn.

Rest your thumb on top of the disc. Grip the rim with your other fingers. Point your right shoulder at your target. Bring the disc back to your left hip.

FUN FACT

Snapping your wrist makes the disc fly a long distance.

FUN FACT

A long pass is called a huck.

Now swing around to face your target. Keep the disc flat, and your eye on your receiver. Spin the disc with a snap of your wrist, and throw!

THE CATCH

You can catch the disc like a sandwich. Clap one hand on top and one on bottom. **Clamp** hard to stop the disc from spinning.

You can also catch the rim with both hands. That is called the **crab claw**.

An Ultimate field is shaped like a rectangle. It is 70 yards (64 m) long. That's shorter than an American football field.

Practice catching with a game of "monkey in the middle." Pass the disc back and forth to a friend. Someone stands in the middle and tries to catch it in the air first.

FUN FACT

Players can't grab a disc out of someone's hands, or knock into a player. No rough play is allowed.

GOOD SPORTS

Teach your friends how to catch and throw. Ultimate players help each other learn—and cheer each other on. Ultimate players are good sports!

FUN FACT

In the 1870s, college students at Yale University tossed empty pie tins around yelling "Frisbie!" The pie tins came from a Connecticut bakery called the Frisbie Pie Company.

GLOSSARY

backhand (BAK-hand): The backhand is the most common throw. Players place a thumb on top of the disc and four fingers below. The back of the hand faces the target.

clamp (KLAMP): To clasp your hands down firmly on the disc. Catching the disc this way stops it from spinning. Sweet!

crab claw (KRAB KLAW): This is another name for a two-handed rim catch.

defenders (di-FEND-urz): A defender is someone on the other team who is trying to stop you from passing, catching, or scoring.

disc (DISK): A disc is a thin, round object. An Ultimate disc is made of plastic.

end zone (END ZOHN): Like football, there is an end zone at both ends of an Ultimate field. Teams pass the disc down the field and try make a final catch in the opponent's end zone for one point.

frisbee (FRIZ-bee): A frisbee is another name for a round plastic disc. A toy company named Wham-O makes a disc called a Frisbee. Some people even call the game Ultimate Frisbee.

TO LEARN MORE

In the Library

Hawes, Alison. *My Frisbee*. Crystal Lake, IL: Rigby, 2000.

Parinella. James. *Ultimate Techniques and Tactics*. Champaign, IL: Human Kinetics, 2004.

Sach, Jacqueline. *The Wham-O Ultimate Frisbee Handbook: Tips and Techniques for Playing Your Best in Ultimate Frisbee*. Kennebunkport, ME: Cider Mill Press, 2009.

On the Web

Visit our Web page for lots of links about Ultimate:

childsworld.com/links

Note to parents, teachers, and librarians: We routinely verify our Web links to make sure they are safe, active sites—so encourage your readers to check them out!

INDEX